Quiet Courage

Conquering Fear and Despair

with the

Stockdale Paradox

Healing for Life Series

Book 2

Suzanne Grosser

Copyright © 2016 by Suzanne Grosser

This book is dedicated with love to the memory of my brother, Dave. He deserved better.

"You are braver than you believe, [and] stronger than you seem."

A.A. Milne

Table of Contents

Introduction
The Stockdale Paradox

Author's Notes
About the Author

Introduction

C ourage can be as dramatic as facing down an armed gunman, or dashing into the path of a car to save a puppy. It is the stuff of superheroes, historical legends, and a few individuals whose valor gets splashed across the headlines. It is tweeted, shared, liked, and then thrust aside for the next dramatic story.

This book is not about that type of courage. I admire those brave souls, but I am not one of them. I am more of a flight, rather than fight, kind of girl. That is if I can un-freeze my body enough to move my feet.

I am not a brave person, yet I find a way to do what scares me when I know it has to be done. I am still terrified, holding it together by sheer force of will, but I refuse to quit, usually because I can see no other way through the danger except to face it head on. I do what has to be done. If my hands are shaking, well, most people won't notice.

The Exception

There is one exception to my flight rather than fight predisposition. My children. If you have children, you know what I mean.

Introduction

Growing up, I had an uncle who terrified me. He had never done anything to me but, I was afraid. Despite the reassurances of other adults, I still felt a twisting in my guts when he was around. So, I avoided him - flight! I did nothing to call his attention to me - freeze!

Years later, I attended a family reunion. I was all grown up with two children of my own. I had a baby in my arms, and a toddler at my side. I saw my uncle. He was heading my way. But I was not afraid; I was something altogether different.

The hair on the back of my neck stood up. My eyes narrowed. I could almost feel my lips curling back into a snarl. I did not feel fear. I felt aggression, a desire to pounce and destroy this threat. Whoa! Where did that come from?

The arrogant smirk he always had for me, slid off his face. He changed direction. He never spoke to me. He never got any closer to me or my children, and I never let them out of my sight until we left.

Was he a threat? I don't know. But I know I was not going to find out at the expense of my children. I don't know if that is courage. It might have been a combination of instinct and priorities. But I never considered any other course of action than fighting against that threat to my children.

Introduction

Brave People

I am grateful that there are those people who are both brave and strong, people who are willing to be heroes. I am grateful that there are people who wake up every morning, willing to rush into a burning building, walk a beat, or stand guard duty. Knowing they exist makes me feel safer in this world. They can inspire us all to stand a little taller when facing our own fight.

But as I said, this book is not about that kind of courage. This book is about a less dramatic type of courage. It is about getting up every morning and facing what needs to be faced. This courage battles demons and fights against larger-than-life foes. Hopeless odds. Altered bodies. Ruined relationships.

Quiet Courage

Financial disasters. This is the courage to quietly take small steps in the right direction, every single day, despite the seeming impossibility of ever reaching your goal.

There is not a lot of public recognition for this everyday struggle: facing obstacles and making tough choices. This kind of courage is not something you do once. You choose it over and over again. You do it alone, without praise or a cheering section.

You do not want to get out of bed, but you get out of bed. You feed the baby. You do the laundry. You go to work. You look for work. You deal with the financial disaster, the devastating illness, or the dissolving relationship that has become the center of your life. You do it knowing that the progress

Introduction

you make today may be lost by the time you wake tomorrow. You do it knowing that you will get up tomorrow anyway, and do it all over again.

That is Quiet Courage. This book will help you develop the inner strength to practice this type of courage.

Quiet Courage is getting up every morning and facing the hell that your life has become.

Quiet Courage is dealing with your own pain, yet choosing to smile at strangers, coworkers, and other innocent bystanders.

Quiet Courage is calling up a friend and saying, "Tell me something good that is happening in your life."

Quiet Courage

Quiet Courage is asking for help when you need it. It is being grateful for those who say yes and understanding of those who say no.

If you or someone you love has experienced a trauma, you need this type of courage. You need an inner strength you may not know you possess. It is there. I will help you find it. Equally important, I will help you take the first steps toward rebuilding your life. To do that, we need to talk about Admiral James Stockdale.

I was introduced to Admiral Stockdale's story at a time when my life was in turmoil and I really couldn't see how it would ever get better. His philosophy has become known as

Introduction

the Stockdale Paradox. That philosophy helped me survive and ultimately, thrive.

I hope this book strengthens and inspires you to face the challenges in your life.

"To fear is one thing,
to let fear grab you by the tail
and swing you around is another."

Katherine Patterson

The Stockdale Paradox

Admiral James Stockdale spent eight years in a Vietnamese prison camp. He was tortured, starved, and constantly threatened with death. He never knew if today was the day he would be tortured to death, or if it was the day they would all be set free. As it turned out, the day he was set free, he had to be carried on a stretcher because the damage done to his body made it impossible for him to walk.

As the highest ranking imprisoned officer, Admiral Stockdale was responsible not only for himself, but for the other prisoners as well. He took this duty seriously. Talk about an impossible task! How could he hope to lead others in a situation where he himself was nearly powerless?

Yet he did just that. He led courageously. He inspired the other prisoners, he gave them direction and hope, but not a false hope. He taught them to grab every shred of power they had, however small. He taught them to see the truth without losing heart. He lived the wisdom that has come to be known as the Stockdale Paradox:

The Stockdale Paradox

*Retain faith that you will prevail in the end,
regardless of the difficulties*

and at the same time

*Confront the most brutal facts of your current
reality, whatever they might be.*

Quiet Courage

This is not a "don't worry, be happy" philosophy.

It is not "hang in there, everything will be fine" advice.

Admiral Stockdale was worried. Everything was not fine. If your family is recovering from trauma, you should be worried. Everything is not fine. But he prevailed, and so can you.

You have to see what is there; confront the brutal facts. Admiral Stockdale did. But he never lost hope. And neither should you.

You can never afford to lose hope. Retain faith that you will prevail, despite your brutal reality. See what is there. Believe you can win. Although it seems impossible, you must do both of those things, and do them at the same time. This applies no matter how dire your situation.

The first part of this book focuses on the first part of the paradox: keeping the faith that you will prevail. The odds are against you, but you can thrive. This is not false hope. It is not the belief in a miracle rescue. It is the faith that YOU will prevail. You will not lose yourself. Stockdale might have died in that prison camp, but he still would have prevailed because he never lost himself. Remain true to who you are and no matter what else is taken from you, you will prevail. Do not surrender yourself.

The second part of this book tackles the second part of the paradox: confronting the most brutal facts of your current reality. It takes real courage to see things are they are. But if you refuse to see the truth, however ugly, you have no power to change any of it. Stockdale did not shrink from his reality. For that reason, he was able to seize what little power he had and use it to improve his situation and lead the other prisoners. You have to be open to the truth to find your power within it.

PART 1

*Retain faith that you will prevail in the end,
regardless of the difficulties.*

"The biggest abuse of power is not owning it."

Nancy Santo Pietro

"Faith is stepping out into the unknown with nothing to guide us, but a hand just beyond our grasp."

Frederick Buechner

Retain Faith

You may be the victim of illness, economics, violence, or just bad luck, but your pain is real. Whatever you are facing, you will not overcome this disaster if you lose faith. If you give into despair you will have no energy and no reason to get up each morning and try again.

Regardless of the impossibilities that you confront, you have to hold tightly to faith in your ultimate triumph. It might not be today, but it will happen. You need that faith. It is your light. You cannot master the dark if you do not believe in the light.

You want to be strong enough to fight back, to survive, and to thrive. You want to be happy again. You know if you can get through this, you will be happy again. Your family will have good times again. In the dark hours, it can be hard to trust the light. But you must.

You need faith if you are to prevail. You need a vision of a good life, after this tragedy. You need to believe in a future you want or you will give up. You will lose the resolve to keep going. Without faith, there is only dark. With faith, even though you are surrounded by dark, you know the light exists.

Retain Faith

This faith does not mean that things will go the way you want. Cancer may win. The bank may take your house. You may lose precious things. You may lose people who matter. But the best part of you will survive. The ones you love and lose, forever remain a part of your soul.

The light exists. You carry it within you.

This first section of the book contains five ways to shore up your faith when you want to quit.

"I submit to you that if a man hasn't discovered something he will die for, he isn't fit to live."

Martin Luther King Jr.

"It takes more bravery to wield ones' values proudly, than to wield arms."

Unknown.

What is Important?

There is always something to fear. Most people have lists of things that disturb and intimidate them. My list is embarrassingly long. Spiders, snakes, rats, especially rats. Anything that comes flying at me, no matter how benign. Yes, I have flinched because of a butterfly. Yes, my friends laughed at me.

You have your own list. Use your list! You can beat one fear by finding a bigger one. Your fears are probably ranked in importance by what they could take from you. You are probably more afraid of tigers than roaches. The tiger could take your life. The roach only threatens your cleanliness, and probably grosses you out. Or maybe that's just me.

Because your life is more valuable to you than being spotlessly clean, tigers are scarier than roaches. You can squash a roach and sanitize the counter, but only if you are alive. If the tiger gets you, the roaches won't matter.

If you know what is most important to you, you can find the courage within your fears. Most people fear losing their money, but if their child was missing, they would spend every dime and borrow more, to find

What is Important?

that child. They value the child more than any fortune.

You might not be able to change your current dire situation. You have much at risk. Be clear about what you value, about what matters most, and you will take action to preserve that. You will lose something. That is a brutal fact, but you can prevail. Put your efforts into preserving what matters most.

Difficult Choices

Face your fear. Do not sacrifice what is most precious, even if doing so would allow you to escape this pain. Stand and fight. You will sacrifice the less important for what you value most. In the end, you will prevail because you did not give up what you truly valued.

What do you value most? Take time to consider this. Your future depends on the answer.

Dave's story

I want to share my brother's story here. Maybe it will help you save what matters most to you.

My brother Dave died because he refused to face the brutal fact that there was a contract out on his life. He had helped the police put a drug dealer in jail. That drug dealer had a brother, who stepped into his place. Business continued and my brother was a marked man.

What is Important?

Once he gave up the street life, Dave was invisible to the drug community. But when he chose to get completely clean, he knew he needed help to get off the prescription oxycodone. He decided to attend Cocaine Anonymous (CA).

It was a reasonable choice, a good plan with only one flaw. People convicted of drug violations are routinely ordered by the courts to attend CA. My brother was there voluntarily. A lot of other people were not.

One of those court-ordered attendees recognized Dave and knew there was a price on his head. I don't know how much that person was paid, but it was blood money.

After the next meeting, three thugs followed Dave home. At the time, he was living with our parents. My brother's life was saved that night by our parents' presence. It would have been bad for business to kill two elderly people in their safe suburban neighborhood home. So his enemies waited.

There were a few more warnings. His vehicle was sabotaged. He had it repaired. He was sideswiped while driving on a major highway and forced into the path of an oncoming tractor-trailer. My brother should have left town, but he didn't. He owned a home and the renter's lease was up. He wanted to move back into his own home. He moved in on Monday. By Friday, he was dead.

If he had faced the brutal facts, he would have walked away from the property. He would have defaulted on the mortgage, left town, and began life anew somewhere else.

Maybe he had information I didn't. Maybe our parents would have been in danger. Perhaps he sacrificed himself to protect our parents. I don't know. I never will. I hope he made the right choice because I miss him.

Dr. Martin Luther King Jr.

Martin Luther King Jr. feared physical harm to his children, but he feared more a world where his children would never be accepted for who they were. He feared that his children would be forced to live tiny, proscribed lives hemmed in by fear. He wanted them to be safe and he wanted them to express their fullest potential.

So he did what he believed to be right and faced the hatred and violence that resulted. He worried for his children's physical safety, as any father would. He knew his own life was in jeopardy. But he did not stop. He continued to speak out, to press for justice. His biggest fear was that he would leave behind a world that had not changed. He valued his children's freedom more than his own life.

In the end, his activism did cost him his life. He was murdered for speaking out, for not compromising his principles. He died for what he believed in, for what he held most precious. As a result, he left behind a bigger

What is Important?

world for his children, a world with more opportunities. Not a perfect world, for sure, but a better one than they would have had if he had stayed quiet and taken the safe, comfortable path.

"I am not afraid . . . I was born to do this."

Joan of Arc

"There is nothing wrong with being afraid, as long as you don't let it change who you are."

Grandma, Paranorman (2012)

Who Will You Be?

Who do you want to be?

You probably know who everyone else wants you to be. Your parents. Your teachers. Your boss. Your pastor. Your lover. They all have a vision of who you should be.

All your life, someone else has been telling you who to be. You comply as a child because you love and trust your parents and teachers. You rebel a bit as a teen, maybe. But you believe that your pastor has good intentions. You accept that your spouse wants the best for you.

The media, especially television, shows us the "ideal" we should aspire to. How we should look. What we should wear. How we should think. We are molded by the people and images around us.

But is that who you want to be? Really? Good for you if it is. But what if it is not?

In the difficult times you are facing, your resolve depends on being totally committed to who you are. Being true to yourself is what will get you through this. You cannot be true to a false image of yourself. You might have been able to fake it while things were going well enough. But you don't have the energy to waste on something you are not. Not anymore.

Be honest about who you are. The real you is worth the fight. Be you. Do whatever it is that your best self would do. People will not always treat you as you deserve, but you can always act as the person you want to be.

It is time to be the person you always intended. You will not please everyone. This will require more courage than you have ever needed before. Be prepared to lose friends. Be prepared to learn who really loves you, not their image of you. In the end, you will prevail and you will find yourself surrounded by people who like you, the real you.

Who do you want to be?

Tatyana McFadden

Spina Bifida is a birth defect where the bones of the spine do not completely form together. It causes a host of problems. Depending on the severity of the defect, the child may have difficulty breathing, controlling bladder and bowels. They usually have some problems with walking and other movements. The most severe cases result in paralysis, and can mean a lifetime in a wheelchair. A baby born with spina bifida faces tough challenges. When that baby is alone, growing up in a Russian orphanage, she is not likely to survive for long. She will probably have a small, short life.

36

Who Will You Be?

But Tatyana McFadden did not know that. The infant survived her early years in the orphanage with its limited resources. When she was six years old, her situation changed for the better. She was fortunate enough to be adopted. With a family of her own, her chances greatly improved. But the battle was not over. Even with a loving family, a supportive home, and excellent medical care, she was not expected to live beyond her teens.

Tatyana had a big spirit and a big dream. She survived against the odds. Now she wanted to live against the odds. Her goal was to be an Olympian. She knew who she wanted to be and she was willing to do whatever it took to make that happen.

Quiet Courage

Because she was committed to her goal, she didn't do the bare minimum of physical therapy. She worked harder than she needed to work. She trained harder than she needed to train. She set goals and she worked toward them. She did not quit.

She did become an athlete. She became an incredibly tough competitor. By pushing herself to the limit, she reached her goal. She won that gold.

In 2012, she won a gold medal in the Paralympics. She accomplished this not by ignoring her limitations. Her need for a wheelchair could not be ignored. She accepted those challenges. She found a way around and through them to her goal. The odds were stacked against her. But she refused to let

Who Will You Be?

those odds overwhelm her. She stayed true to herself, did the work, and fulfilled her dream.

"Forgo prudence in favor of courage."

Sue Monk Kidd

"Courage is the price life exacts for granting peace."

Amelia Earhart

The Power of Regret

I f you have ever felt the sting of regret, congratulations! That means you have principles and a conscience. You know what matters to you, what kind of person you want to be. The pain of your failure, that regret, can now be a powerful tool to keep you going.

You already know what is important to you. Your experience with regret means you know how bad it will feel if you violate your own values. Regret is the result of failing to keep faith with yourself.

Take a minute to think about your biggest regret. Ugh, I know, but bear with me. Let the memory have you for a bit, really feel it.

If you had tried a little harder, or had a little more courage, would it have turned out differently? Could you have changed the outcome? You made choices. Now, you have regrets.

Maybe you lost faith in yourself. Maybe you gave into fear. Maybe you let the darkness win.

Maybe you did your best, but it was not enough. That happens. You made choices you can still respect today, but it didn't turn out the way you had hoped. You feel the regret, but it does not burn quite so deeply. It hurts, but you know you did all you could. You may have failed, but you do not need to feel shame.

Today you will make choices. Maybe only small ones. Small choices may be the only ones you have left. When your life is turned upside down by trauma, much of your power vanishes. You may only have small choices. But that does not mean they are insignificant.

Years from now, when you look back on today, you will want to respect the choices you made. You will want to know that you did all you could. It won't always be easy to do the right thing, but your future depends on the choices you make today.

As I write this now, what I really want to be doing is relaxing in front of the television. I put in a full day at work and that couch is looking oh-so-inviting! But if I do that, this book will never get published. And all those books in my head that I want to write when this one is finished, they won't get published either. That would be a huge regret for me. I don't want that tomorrow, so I stay at the keyboard today.

Today you can choose your best self. You can choose what is most important to you and for your future. Imagine how you will feel in five, ten, or twenty years if you choose anything less than your absolute best today.

The Power of Regret

Keep true to yourself. Keep faith that you will prevail.

What will you do today to avoid a lifetime of regret?

Dakota Meyer

Dakota Meyer is the first living Marine to receive the Medal of Honor since the Vietnam War. During the Battle of Ganjgal, his unit was under attack by Afghan rebels. He was ordered to sit tight, even though four fellow American service members were trapped and in danger. He was ordered to do nothing, to wait and see what happened. He was ordered to stay safe.

He chose to risk both his life and a court martial by disobeying that order and attempting their rescue. Each time he progressed toward their position, others would need his help. He assisted all those who needed him. He brought them back to safety.

Then he went back for his comrades, again. He made multiple attempts, repeatedly risking his life. He was wounded, returned to safety with more refugees from the battle. Despite his injuries, he went back in the line of fire yet again. He saved the lives of 36 people that day, but he could not save his friends. The four trapped Americans died.

He did not have to do this brave thing, in fact he was ordered not to. But he knew himself. He knew that he would regret obeying that order more than the consequences of his disobedience. He was not able to save all, but he saved many. He could not save their lives, but he was able to bring back their bodies for a proper burial. He did not leave them to their enemies. He can hold his head high, knowing he gave his best. He never has to doubt his own courage.

"*[There is a] solitude so deep that you can hear a pin drop at the bottom of your soul. The brave let it bounce and abide.*"

Anneli Rufus

"*We have to be the masters of our imagination, not the prisoners.*"

Thomas Friedman

Set Your Focus

Meditation can help. If you belong to an organized religion, you may choose the form of meditation commonly called prayer. Meditation is a quieting of the mind that relaxes the spirit. Prayer does this by focusing the mind on a benevolent higher power, allowing a release of tension.

The key to meditation is to keep your obsessive, worried, overactive, "monkey mind" quiet. This breaks the grip of stress and fear, letting you think more clearly.

Prayer or meditation calms the spirit and is soothing to the body. It can lower blood pressure and relieve tension. It brings focus to your life. But only if it is the right kind of prayer.

The wrong kind of prayer will sink you deeper into the quicksand of your repetitive thoughts. It will reinforce your fears and obliterate your hope. Pray right!

Don't whine and complain.

Yes, I know your life sucks. If you are praying to a higher power, he/she already knows it, too. Set your attention on the beauty in life, on the good things you still have. Those flowers in your neighbor's yard, the breath in your lungs. Notice and appreciate what is here now.

Don't ask for other people to change.

Of course they should. But don't you have your own faults to work on?

Don't beat yourself up.

You do not deserve this pain. Life did not single you out for this. You are not being punished. Your situation might be the result of choices you made in the past. But today you can make different choices.

Do seek yourself.

You are all you have. You can choose who you want to be. Relax and open to possibilities for a new you.

Get to know your best self. Focus on who you are, on your soul or spirit, and its connection to others. What do you have to offer the world? That is how you will find the path you must take. You will know the way to serve others by being true to yourself.

Do aim for the quiet courage to face your life.

You have the chance now to create a new life with your new choices. But only if you are willing to see where you are right now and what you are facing. That takes courage.

Where will you set your focus today?

Kate Chopin

Kate Chopin was a late 19th-century writer. Her troubles began at the age of 5 when her beloved father sent her away to boarding school. He valued education and wanted the best for his daughter, but Kate was furious at the separation. In the words of her biographer Emily Toth, "for a writer, it was a fine and angry start." Two months later, her father died, the pain between them unresolved.

She became a teenager during the civil war. At the time, she lived in St Louis, a city whose residents were divided in their support between the confederacy and the union. It was a violent and dangerous place for a young almost-woman. When it was over, she spent several years in seclusion, withdrawn from the world, avoiding social situations. No one knows for certain what she experienced during that volatile time, but those are the actions of a traumatized young woman.

Kate chose to be resilient. She married happily. Then, once again, tragedy struck. At the age of 32, she lost her love. She was left with six young children to support. She quickly discovered that the family was bankrupt. She did not live in a time that appreciated self-sufficient women, yet she had no desire to remarry.

She chose to write. She wrote with honesty and honesty is not always appreciated. Her work was not appreciated when it did not conform to proper social standards of the time. But she kept writing.

Set Your Focus

She learned to run a small business and manage money. She supported herself and her children. And she kept writing.

The traumas of her life did not dampen her spirit or ruin her resolve. She shared her gift for words and the gift has become more appreciated as time has passed and new readers discover her work.

"Courage is fear holding on a minute longer."

General George S. Patton

"Courage does not always roar. Sometimes courage is the quiet voice at the end of the day saying, I will try again tomorrow."

Mary Anne Radmacher

Embrace Change

Change is both continuous and inevitable. You cannot stop things from changing. But you can direct the course of that change.

You go to the gym one day and lift weights. Your muscles grow, a little. So little, you do not see it. But if you go to the gym every day for a year and lift weights, you will see a difference. The improvement will become obvious. Too bad most of us give up because, in the beginning, the changes are so small. We want instant results and that is not how the world works.

You can turn this to your advantage. You probably cannot make huge changes today, but you will make little ones. Your energy will grow and you will move slowly in the direction you want to go. You will gain momentum and power over time. You will see the improvement. Probably not today, but you will see it eventually.

Your life will be changed by the choices you make today. It may be difficult to see the little differences your choice might make, but it is happening. Will you skip physical therapy, or go and give it your best? Will you have another cigarette? Will you make the decision today to forgive your attacker? Will you let go of your need to blame someone else for your problems? Will you ask for the help you need?

Change is inevitable, and sometimes it is out of our control. Cells turn cancerous. Cures do not work. Sometimes you have little power. But if you believe in yourself, when an opportunity presents itself, you will recognize it as your chance. If you take an active part, you can choose the direction that change will take.

Whatever you are facing in your life, it is changing even as you read this. How will you direct that change?

Astou

A young French woman named Astou, was being physically abused by her husband. Besides being beaten, she and her children were routinely locked in their apartment. He frequently withheld even basic necessities such as food and water. She continued to nurse her infant even as she herself was undernourished and becoming dehydrated.

Then things got worse. After a violent attack by her husband, neighbors called the police. This should have been her rescue. Instead, her husband convinced authorities that she was the abuser. She was tried, convicted, and sent to jail. Talk about life not being fair!

Embrace Change

She could have given in to despair. She could have sought revenge for her pain. But she knew who she was, and she saw this awful turn of events as an opportunity for change. She was confined to a jail cell, instead of an apartment, but that meant she was no longer isolated and controlled by her husband.

She accepted the counseling and help that was offered to her while she was incarcerated. She learned about PADV, Partnership Against Domestic Violence. This organization became her salvation. They provided her with the resources and emotional support she needed to regain her children and to escape her violent husband.

Quiet Courage

Instead of seeing herself as a victim, she recognized her own inner strength. Motivated by the value she placed on saving her children, she grabbed at every bit of help she could. It took a jail sentence to set her free, and she was not going to miss the opportunity.

Part 2

Confront the most brutal facts of your current reality, whatever they might be.

*"A cobra will bite you whether you call it
cobra or Mr. Cobra."*

Indian Proverb

*"Every sinner has a future,
Every saint has a past."*

Anonymous

Confront Reality

You have faith in your heart. You know what is important to you and you know who you want to be. You are strong enough to make the right choices, no matter how difficult that becomes. You are determined and focused.

Whatever the outcome, you are not going to lose yourself. You have chosen to stand firm for yourself and to remain faithful to your most precious, deeply-held values.

Quiet Courage

This situation will change. It might take a long time. Things could get worse before they get better. But you will prevail. Now it is time to accept how difficult that will be.

It is awesome to know that you will make it past this trying time in your life. The trauma of the past will not control the future. Your faith will get you through this, but only if you face the truth.

Your faith will not save you if you refuse to face the bitter, brutal, truth. It sounds harsh. It is harsh, but it is true. Now is the time to face the reality of your situation. Look at your circumstances and your resources, no matter how limited. You might be afraid, or feel overwhelmed. That's okay. That is part of your truth, too.

Confront Reality

You must be not only willing but determined, to see what is and act upon those facts. It takes strength of character like you have never needed before. Your situation is full of pain and opportunity. You cannot see the second if you shut your eyes tight against the first. It takes courage to look the ugly truth in the eye and not turn away.

You may have set out on this journey not realizing the courage it would require of you, or this path may have been thrust upon you. But the means to surmount the difficulties are the same, beginning with facing the brutal facts.

Keeping your faith while honestly facing reality is how you find the little bits of power you have within this situation. You have to see the whole picture, even the parts you would much rather not look at, to find the way through this mess. That is the value of the second half of the Stockdale Paradox.

It is about finding your power, however limited. Only the truth can do that. The truth may not be pretty. It may not be what you want to see. But it is the truth.

Once you are honest with yourself about what is impossible, then you know that everything else is possible. You may not like your options. You never wanted to be in this position with so little power and so few possibilities. Your choices are limited, but you can still do something. Grab those little bits of power and use them. They may not seem like

Confront Reality

much, but with the faith that you have in your heart, they will be enough.

The next section discusses five ways to strengthen your vision and see the truth.

"Courage is grace under pressure."

Ernest Hemingway

"You must do the thing you think you cannot do."

Eleanor Roosevelt

Abandon False Hope

T he first step before you can change anything is to accept the way things really are.

One of the most surprising observations that Admiral Stockdale made while he was a POW was that hope can kill. He watched men die as their hope evaporated and their spirit gave up. This sounds like the opposite of having faith that you will prevail, but it is not.

Quiet Courage

The fault was not faith that they would prevail, but false hope. They had imagined they would be released within a month or a season, or by a certain date. They put their faith and hope in that desire. The time would come and go, with no change. The hope had been false and when it died, it took a bit of their will to live.

Admiral Stockdale knew he could not predict when or even if he would be released. He saw the peril of building up hope without cause. The truth was that he could not know how long he would be imprisoned. He could not know if he would survive his imprisonment. That is a brutal reality.

Accept things as they are. Do not lie to yourself.

Abandon False Hope

You want to believe that something will magically change your situation. Instead of having to file bankruptcy, you will hit the lottery. Your abusive spouse will see the error of his ways. Your accuser will admit her lies. A cure will be found. You will get your kids back by Christmas. The bank won't foreclose. If your plan relies on incredible good fortune, a complete change of someone's personal character, lost paperwork, or a particular alignment of the stars, it is false hope.

False hope keeps you from doing what you can while you wait for the miracle. After all, if you are going to hit the lottery, why make an appointment for a free bankruptcy consultation? When the miracle does not happen, you are plunged deeper into despair.

Quiet Courage

You have wasted valuable time and the situation has gotten worse. Another month's worth of unpaid bills has stacked up, along with late fees and overdraft charges. You lose the will to fight. You lose your grip on your power. You are less than you could be.

See the truth. You probably won't hit the lottery.

Act within your limitations. Call for that appointment.

Avoid false hope. If the miracle happens, rejoice. Cancel your appointment and pay all your creditors.

But if the miracle never comes, you will not be devastated. You will already be working to solve your problems. When a real opportunity opens up, like a better paying job, you will have the clear vision to see it. And use it to make your situation that much better.

It takes courage to face reality. But if you refuse to see the full truth of your situation, you lose all your power. Do not give up your power. Be brave.

What are you afraid to see in your own situation?

Travis Mills

As a child, Travis Mills was an active small town boy who loved sports. He was always in motion: running and playing. He loved being part of a team, the experience of camaraderie and unity. He loved his town, his family, his friends. That love grew into a loyalty that extended to his country and as an adult he chose to serve in the United States

Quiet Courage

Army. During his third tour of duty in Afghanistan, he was critically injured by an IED. He lost both arms and both legs. He survived, but he has chosen to go beyond mere survival. He has chosen to really live.

He lost not only limbs but the image he had of himself. Fit and athletic all his life, he woke in the hospital unable to care for himself even in the most basic ways. He could have chosen to remain an invalid. Instead, he refused to give up despite the pain, the multiple surgeries, and endless physical therapy.

He suffered with the pain and with depression. This was not easy for him. But he had those deep-rooted values he refused to

Abandon False Hope

deny. He faced his losses and got on with life, bit by bit, savoring each hard won victory.

He challenges himself every day to do the difficult things his recovery requires. He has his fears and his demons. But he also has quiet courage. He remains a loving husband and father. He gets up every morning and he faces what he calls his "new normal."

Quiet Courage

"*Courage is the ability to choose love rather than fear, regardless of circumstances.*"

Steve Pavlina

"*It is never too late to be what you might have been.*"

George Ernst

Emulate a Hero

What you face now may be more difficult than anything else you have ever done, but that does not mean you cannot do it. You have grown strong through the trials and joys of your life. Now you will need all that strength to fight and win this battle.

When your courage is failing, let the bravery of others bolster your own. When you see that others have endured the same, or worse, you gain encouragement. You might even feel a twinge of shame that you are shrinking from this trial after looking at what others have been through. Don't bother with shame. Others have felt the same fear, the same desire to avoid the pain of this fight. They chose to fight, instead of run. You can too.

There is power in knowing you are not the first to face such challenges. Others have walked through this darkness to emerge on the other side. There is life after trauma, life after the ordeal. A different life, no doubt. But a good life, nonetheless.

Let the perseverance of those who have gone before, invigorate you. Let their courage urge you forward. Stand tall. You do not walk alone.

The examples in this book were chosen not only for their courage and persistence in the face of dire circumstances, but for their differences. Some of these heroes are rich, others poor. Some are highly educated, others illiterate. Some had the benefit of loving families while others were not so fortunate. Your circumstances and your background might influence where you are today, but they do not dictate your future. That is up to you.

What is the same about all of the heroes in this book is their spirit. At their core, they have strength and determination that enabled them to prevail. They are ordinary people who showed quiet courage in the face of desperate circumstances. Their particular stories may be different from yours. But the spirit that kept them going is dancing within you.

Knowing that someone else has survived against tremendous odds will lift you up. If they can do it, you know you can. It was not easy for these individuals. They have all suffered their dark moments. Fear and despair knock at everyone's door. But heroes believe in the light, even when the darkness threatens to swallow them whole. Be inspired by these ordinary heroes. Then become one yourself.

Whose courage can you emulate today?

Tina Frundt

Tina Frundt spends her nights on the seedy streets of Washington, D.C., offering hope to sex slaves. Helping them is how she saves herself.

Tina grew up in a series of foster homes. At age 14, she was kidnapped. She was starved, beaten, burned with cigarettes, had her fingers broken, and was gang raped. Repeatedly. For over a year. She was forced to earn a minimum of $500 per night by submitting to sex with strangers.

She "escaped" by being arrested for prostitution. She was 15 years old. Instead of being treated for her wounds, both mental and physical, she was punished with incarceration. When she was released from jail a year later, she had no family and no follow-up services to provide her with counseling, education, or even a place to stay.

Her healing journey has been difficult, full of deep wells of depression. She tells of hitting bottom many times. Yet she has come back. She has an incredible spirit.

Tina has built a new life, not by focusing on herself, but by saving others. Instead of wallowing in her own pain, she seeks to alleviate the suffering of others. She knows the pain of sex slaves. She understands the hell of teens trapped in the abuse and degradation of the sex trade. She offers hope to the victims of today's predators.

Instead of seeking revenge for the injustices of her past, she seeks to educate the public to the reality of the modern-day sex trade in the United States. She works with the Women's Funding Network to spread the word, in hopes of making the world safer for today's children.

Tina started a non-profit organization she named Courtney's House. It runs an on-the-street outreach, a telephone hotline, and a shelter, all giving hope to the desperate. It offers help to sex slaves, the help she herself never received.

Shifting the focus from herself, she uses her horrific experience to motivate her to make the world safer for others. Looking beyond her own pain, Tina found a way to heal herself by healing others.

"It was worth living a difficult life if you had a great aim like that."

Will Parry, The Subtle Knife

"If it scares you, it might be a good thing to try."

Seth Godin

Accept
Responsibility

S ometimes the disaster that befalls you is
a result of bad luck. A storm, an illness,
a bad economy, a drunk driver. You did not
cause these things to happen. But your actions
may still have contributed to the problems
you are facing.

You let your insurance lapse, you
neglected your health, you didn't give your
best at work, you got into a car with a driver

you knew was impaired. Still you did not cause the damage to your home. You did not know you were being exposed to toxins. Your employer failed on its own and how could you truly know the level of your friend's impairment?

There is a fine line between blaming yourself and accepting responsibility for your actions. Blame beats people up. Accepting responsibility frees people up.

Blame is counterproductive.

Accepting responsibility gives you the power to move forward.

I was assaulted by a man I knew. Was I to blame? No, of course not. But did I have responsibility? Sure. My intuition said

Accept Responsibility

something was off about him, but I ignored that tiny voice - until it was too late.

You made choices. They may have been perfectly reasonable at the time, but things did not work out as you anticipated. You cannot change the past, but you can improve your future.

You did not cause the accident, but maybe the reason you could not get the best orthopedic doctor in town to treat your injury is because of that outstanding bill you have refused to discuss with his office.

You let your anger at the injustice of that lousy driver fill your thoughts, and it spills out when your physical therapist is trying to stretch you. Your mental resistance becomes physical resistance.

Quiet Courage

You slack off on the exercises because it is difficult and painful, and really, you should not have to do this! It was not your fault. You should not have to endure this! You are right, but you are making a mistake.

You will suffer if you choose to focus on the injustice of your situation, instead of your power within it.

That is the beauty of responsibility. You can make your life better by accepting responsibility for your choices. Only when you see yourself clearly can you take back your power to make the changes that will improve your life.

You can call the doctor's office and set up a payment plan.

Accept Responsibility

You can give physical therapy your best effort.

I promised myself to always listen to my intuition. I have kept that promise and it has saved me a great deal of anguish. I trust me now.

Forget how it is the other guy's fault; this is your life. The ones who hurt you do not care if you ever get better. They do not care if you are sad or angry. They do not care about you. That is the brutal truth.

You are the only one being hurt by your anger. Even if you were to exact revenge against those who hurt you, it would be at the price of your soul. And they still wouldn't care about you, only about their own pain.

Quiet Courage

Talk to a counselor if necessary to release your anger. But do find a way to let go of it.

You need to let go of your obsession with injustice. Sometimes, life is not fair. Get over it. Get on with it.

Do not sink into blame. Rise to accept responsibility and with that responsibility comes your power. You will get back your life when you take it back. No one is going to come along and fix everything for you. There is no fairy godmother to wave a magic wand and cure your life.

You are responsible for you. You have the most to gain - or lose - from your choices. Take an honest look at what is left to you and decide what life you can make for yourself.

Accept Responsibility

Choose, then act. You are the only one who can do that for you.

How will be true to yourself today?

Dr. Wayne Dyer

If you search for Dr. Wayne Dyer you will find his website, a Wikipedia entry, numerous blog entries, and several biographies. You will learn that he has published over 30 books, created numerous audio-programs, produced a movie, and has made numerous radio and television appearances. You will learn that his work has an international appeal and thousands credit him with vastly improving their life.

But there is another side to Dr. Dyer. You have to dig a little deeper to learn that he grew up in a series of orphanages and foster homes, that he has suffered three failed marriages. He does not hide these facts, but they do not define who he is.

It would be easy for him to blame his failures on his difficult past. Instead, he credits his past with making him more compassionate. He does not harbor resentment or blame others for his painful experiences. He does not excuse his actions as an adult by blaming his childhood fears and isolation.

If you listen to his talks or read his books, what you find is a man who is honest with himself, who moves forward from the point where he is, to make his own life. The pain of his past has been transformed into a desire to heal others. His hard work has brought him self-satisfaction and in the process he has helped many others to achieve their best.

Everyone fails, but not everyone gets back up. You are reading this book so I suspect you are the type that gets back up.

*"Life shrinks or expands in proportion
to one's courage."*

Anais Nin

*"A man with outward courage dares to die;
a man with inner courage dares to live."*

Lao Tzu

96

Forgo Blame

Someone else made a decision that changed your life. It might have been a stranger, or a friend, perhaps a dishonest business partner, or a faithless mate. It might have been a foolish mistake or a conscious choice on their part. It might have been callous self-interest or calculated evil

They caused this change in your life. That may seem to be the objective truth.

Quiet Courage

They are responsible for the mess your life is now. That is a lie.

Whatever anyone else did, your life is always yours to mold. Never give away all of your power by giving in to the idea that someone else can change you.

Betrayal can change your circumstances, financially or emotionally. An injury can curtail your physical abilities. You may have your options limited. Trauma does that. But you are free to make your own choices among the options left to you.

Maybe all you have left within your control is your attitude. Make it your own. Be yourself.

Forgo Blame

Others can hurt you. They can take things from you. But they cannot change who you are. Their actions may change what you can do, but only you can choose to let it change who you are.

Blaming someone else gives them control over your life. You fixate on them, instead of the life you could be making for yourself. Your thoughts are filled with plans and schemes to get even. Most likely, they have long since forgotten all about you. This is why you do not want revenge.

You may be absolutely justified in your anger. You are right! They are wrong! But if you cannot let that go, they become the center of your world. You will spend years pursuing retribution that, in the end will not make you feel any better.

It takes courage to let go of blame and face your life as it is. Be brave.

Who will you stop blaming today?

William McNamara

William McNamara, was an NYPD police officer. He walked a beat, protecting his fellow citizens. Then one day in 1978, a gunshot changed his life. Suddenly, he was paralyzed, unable to walk at all. His life was turned upside down. He was confined to a wheelchair. From power to helplessness in an instant. He had to work hard to physically recover and even harder to focus on creating a new life for himself.

Forgo Blame

He could no longer walk a beat. Instead of focusing on the limitations of his body, he used the abilities he did have. He went to graduate school. He became a detective. He married and had a family.

Years later, the gunman, seeking parole said he felt bad for McNamara and his family. McNamara shrugged it off. He had moved on from that awful moment to create a life for himself. In his own words, "I had a full life."

It would have been easy for McNamara to blame the gunman. He could have chosen anger. He could have spent his days raging over the injustice of losing his mobility. Instead, he chose the more difficult, more courageous path. He claimed power over his life.

*"You have to really grab a hold of yourself,
forget shame, forget what I can't do,
because that was the hardest thing for me."*

James Tremble

*"Faith is taking the first step even when
you don't see the whole staircase."*

Martin Luther King Jr.

Connect with Others

You may be overwhelmed by the difficulties you face. Who wouldn't be? Everything has changed. New challenges appear each day. Things that once were easy, are now difficult.

It can feel like too much to handle alone. Yet, you feel isolated and afraid. You know you need help, but to ask for help seems so weak! You berate yourself for not being stronger.

Quiet Courage

You are ashamed of your situation and your perceived failures. The more your own actions led to this catastrophe, the more guilt and shame you will experience. Even if you did not cause this problem, you still feel that somehow, you should have known it was coming. You should have been prepared to escape it or you should deal with it without bothering everyone you know with your whining and complaints.

Stop. It happened. You are doing your best now. It is okay to need help.

It will be easier if you realize you are not the only one facing such hardships. One of the things Admiral Stockdale did while imprisoned was to devise a system of communication among the prisoners in the

Connect With Others

camp. Their captors had isolated the men from one another as a tool of control. Stockdale wanted to unite them.

When Stockdale created a system of communication that his captors could not detect, it gave the men hope. This covert ability to connect with other prisoners was a tiny assertion of power. It did not change any part of their circumstances except the knowledge that they were not alone. They were connected. They were in this together. It gave them strength to endure. It helped them survive.

There are resources out there, for whatever trauma you are facing. You will have to seek them out. You have to take that first step of reaching out for what you need.

105

Quiet Courage

That may be the most difficult part, the reaching out. It means opening your pain and your failures for others to see. Going to AA means admitting you have a problem with alcohol. Meeting with a PTSD support group means admitting you are not invincible.

Often people associate asking for help with weakness. The opposite is true. It is scary to drop your "perfect life" mask that everyone wears and let the truth out for all the world to see. It is terrifying to be vulnerable. It takes courage to ask for help.

If you join a support group, you will be giving, as well as receiving support. Together with others who understand the challenges you face, you grow stronger. You can help others and yourself at the same time. And that will make you feel better about yourself.

Right now, you are down and you need help. You have to find the courage to overcome your fear and your shame. There are hands outstretched waiting to grasp yours and help you up. Reach out for the support you need.

Who could you reach out to today?

James Tremble

James Tremble dropped out of school in the fourth grade. He was behind his classmates academically and getting further behind each year. He was born into a time and place where a person could function without an extended education.

Quiet Courage

His lack of education did limit his options. Perhaps he would never be a community leader, or a doctor, or the head of a corporation, but other doors were open to him. He was friendly and sociable. He had an excellent memory and a gift for organizing information. He used these talents to build a career as a DJ. He used the image on each disk to identify the songs on it.

He had never learned to read in school and he hid that fact from those around him. For over 50 years, he lived with this personal embarrassment and a sense of his own failure. The world was changing around him. He saw opportunities pass him by. Eventually, he came out of hiding. He decided it was time to

Connect With Others

get the education he had missed out on so many years before.

He swallowed his pride and went to his local nonprofit literacy council. There, he found compassion and the help he needed to learn to read. It was not easy. He had to work hard. It took time, but he persisted. His tutors both encouraged and challenged him. It happened slowly but the words came and the world opened up to him.

He had never participated in politics because he could not read the newspapers or even read a voter's ballot. But once he learned to read, that changed. At the age of 65, for the first time in his life, James Tremble exercised his right to vote.

"We feel endlessly distant,
though we are endlessly bound by love."

Rainer Renee Rilke

"Have patience with all things,
but first of all with yourself."

St. Francis de Sales

A Note on Depression

If you are depressed, you may find the suggestions in this book difficult if not impossible, to implement. Depression is not laziness, nor is it a lack of willpower. Depression is screwed up chemistry in your brain.

Depression can be situational or chronic.

Situational depression means your life sucks and you are overwhelmed by all the crap you have to deal with. It might be caused by recent events that are pushing you to the limits of your resources. There is simply too much to do and you don't know where to begin. You have lost so much, you see no reason to try anymore, you just want to curl up under the covers and stay there.

Chronic depression is the type that has been with you a really, really long time. Chronic depression is a state of mind that feels like it has always been with you. And it feels like it will never go away. It seems your entire life, you have looked at other people and wondered what they were so damned happy about. You may have learned to deal with life by pretending to share in the joy, but you rarely feel it.

A Note About Depression

Both of these forms of depression are serious illnesses and should be treated by a doctor.

Situational depression will probably lift once you get your life issues sorted out. The problem is, depression is destroying your will and sapping your energy. You struggle to take the steps you know you need to take. You don't have the drive to move forward because depression has you stuck in neutral.

You don't want to take meds because you know it will get better. You really don't like the idea of taking medications, especially ones that make other people wonder if you're crazy. You are not crazy. You just need a little help. Talk to your doctor. A short term course of 3 months, 6 months, or even a year, of antidepressant medications, could be the boost you need to get moving again. As you use your newfound energy to take action, your life will improve. Ultimately, you won't need the meds and your momentum will continue to carry you forward.

Chronic depression may require longer term medication. Remember your brain has been set to sad for so long, it is hard to change that setting. If your pancreas was damaged and you had diabetes, you would take insulin to regulate the chemistry of your blood. If you suffer from chronic depression, you probably need medication to regulate the chemistry of your brain. It is a medical treatment that could dramatically change your life.

A Note About Depression

See www.depressionscreen.org for confidential screening to assess whether you need professional help.

If you are depressed, please talk to your doctor about it. Get the help you need to recover from trauma. It takes courage to admit you need help. Be brave. Ask for help.

"He had been to the dungeon and back up out of it.
He knew things they would never know;
what they thought of him, he realized,
did not matter, not at all."

Kate DiCamillo.

Conclusion

Life happens. Things do not go as planned. Accidents change bodies. Death comes too soon. You lose a job, a house, a lover. Difficult economic times force you into situations you hate. People love you; then they don't. Promises are broken. Dreams die.

The future you were working toward, has vanished in the blink of an eye. You don't know what is to come. You aren't sure if want to find out. You can think of many possibilities and none of them are as good as what was lost. You can't see much farther than your deep pain and loss in this moment.

You feel like quitting. You have a right to quit! You don't deserve this!

Quiet courage means digging down, deep inside (some days way, way deep inside) to find that voice that says, "No. I will fight."

It is difficult, but you keep faith in yourself. You know who you are. You know what you want. You are exhausted, but you keep going. You are beaten, but not defeated. You have values that are important, and giving up is not one of them. You have a place in this world, a voice that needs to be heard. You matter.

Conclusion

You may not know yet what the purpose of your life is. You thought you did, but then everything changed. Once you get through this - and you will get through this - you may find your purpose has changed. Perhaps that change has grown out of this difficult time.

For many people, their suffering motivates them to help others in pain. Some, like Dr. Martin Luther King Jr., work to prevent others from being hurt in the same way they were. Dr. King worked to give others opportunities he never had. Some, like Tina Frundt, focus on rescuing those who are already in trouble. She is successful because she can relate to those hurting teens with full understanding.

Quiet Courage

Your willingness to grow through your trauma can be an inspiration to others. You might be exactly the example someone else needs to see. What you learn could be the wisdom that saves another from suffering.

Don't quit. The world needs you.

Quiet Courage is not being fearless. Fearless is often simply foolish. Quiet Courage is facing what you fear. You may surprise yourself with how brave you can be. Here are a few lines about one of my favorite characters in Kate DiCamillo's book, *The Tale of Despereaux.*

*"Despereaux marveled at his own bravery.
He admired his own defiance.
And then, reader, he fainted."*

Conclusion

Always marvel at your own bravery, even if you faint. Then pull yourself back up. That is the immense power of Quiet Courage.

Do You Need Help?

For help with domestic violence:

www.thehotline.org

For help with veterans' issues:

www.veteranscrisisline.net

For resources to prevent suicide:

www.save.org

Author Notes

Thank you for choosing me to walk this healing journey with you.

www.authorsuzannegrosser.com

Share the Love

If this book has helped you, please let others know. Recommend it to your friends, share it on your favorite social media, or give a copy as a gift to someone in need. Maybe all three.

About the Author

P TSD has always been a part of my life. I am not a doctor, or a minister, or a counselor. I have no certificates or letters after my name that qualify me to write about trauma. What I do have is a lifetime of experience with post-traumatic stress.

I grew up with parents who suffered from PTSD. That is not what they called it then; it was not called anything. I was incredibly fortunate to always have someone in my life who sheltered me and offered me a different view of the world.

When I learned to read, my world expanded even further. I met many heroes, both real and fictional, who taught me about the world and about myself.

In college, I learned to love research. I found more heroes. One day, in the pages of a book, I met Admiral James Stockdale. That was the beginning of this book.

I hope the things that I learned from my experience will be useful to you. I hope my words will help you recover faster or avoid some pitfalls. My goal is not to tell you what to do or how to fix your life. My goal is to support your autonomy in choosing the life you want to live and the person you want to be.

Acknowledgments

I want to thank Jim Collins of www.jimcollins.com for introducing the Stockdale Paradox to the world in his book, *Good to Great.* Of course, Admiral Stockdale's willingness to share his experience in his own book, *In Love and War,* gave Jim Collins the story to begin his research. Collins developed this philosophy from it, which he then applied to business. We all build on the work of one another.

I want to thank all the brave soldiers who were the first to share the life-changing nature of experiencing trauma. Whether it was called "shell-shock" or "soldier's heart" or "combat fatigue," their willingness to be open about their pain, paved the way for the research and treatments we have today to help all trauma victims. There is much more to be learned, but we move forward with each generation.

I want to thank Paula Ray for her incredible patience as we worked on the cover design, and for her unflagging support of my dreams.

Thank you to MDS for the nifty "jpg to word to pdf" tactic, and to Ben for being on "format emergency standby."

Quiet Courage

To my proofreaders, thank you and bless your tired eyes! Any errors you find are all mine.

To Write Club and Scribe Tribe: Writing can be a lonely business. I am glad for your companionship along the way.

I want to thank the many people who personally touched my life with their love and support. There were teachers who encouraged me and writing partners who challenged me. There were loyal friends and ones who betrayed my trust. They all taught me about who I want to be.

Most important is my heartfelt gratitude for my family. They are both my support and my motivatior

53324816R00078

Made in the USA
San Bernardino, CA
13 September 2017